Survivor Prayers

Talking with God about Childhood Sexual Abuse

Catherine J. Foote

Westminster/John Knox Press
Louisville, Kentucky

Book design by Drew Stevens
Cover design by Susan Brown

First edition

Published by Westminster/John Knox Press
Louisville, Kentucky

This book is printed on acid-free paper that meets the American National Standards Institute Z39.48 standard. ∞

PRINTED IN THE UNITED STATES OF AMERICA
9 8 7 6 5 4 3 2 1

Library of Congress Cataloging-in-Publication Data

Foote, Catherine J., date.
    Survivor prayers : talking with God about childhood sexual abuse /
Catherine J. Foote. — 1st ed.
        p.   cm.
    ISBN 0-664-25435-7 (alk. paper)
    1. Adult child sexual abuse victims—Prayerbooks and devotions–
English.   2. Spiritual life—Christianity.   I. Title.
BV4596.A25F66   1994
242'.6—dc20   93-44220

Avalon Recovery Society
#101 - 1548 Johnston Rd.
White Rock, B.C.
V4B 3Z6

Survivor Prayers

Contents

God Who Walks with Us 36

Acknowledgments

Writing this book has been just one part of an ongoing journey that has taken me to surprising and amazing places. Many have walked with me on the way. I want particularly to acknowledge the contributions of my editors at Westminster/John Knox Press: Alexa Smith, who first suggested the project, and Stephanie Egnotovich, who saw it to completion. I also appreciate the courageous survivors of childhood sexual abuse across the country who have shared their stories with me and stretched my spirit. And especially I thank Annie Riley, who has listened to my own travel tales for a long time. This book is dedicated to Eileen McDaniel, who had to leave too soon, and to Wanda Hestian, who just couldn't stay.

Introduction: A Spiritual Journey

Right by the house where I grew up, there was a ditch where I used to catch tadpoles. We called them pollywogs. I would take a tin can or an old jar—anything I could find. I would climb over the chainlink fence. It had barbed wire on the top, designed to keep us kids out. For me the wire only enhanced the adventure, inviting me to test my skill as I carefully placed hands and feet between the barbs. I would drop down into the ditch and scoop up the pollywogs with their wiggly round bodies and tails. Then, squeezing the jar through a hole in the fence and scaling the fence again, I would return home with my catch.

I would put the pollywogs in a tilted pan, with water at one end. As days and weeks passed, the little creatures would begin to change. First they grew back legs, then front ones, as their tails shrank. Then they would be hopping up out of the water and onto the land, and then one morning they would be gone, hopping back to their home.

This is my image of change. This is metamorphosis. Not the caterpillar, hiding away in the luxurious privacy of a cocoon to become a beautiful butterfly, but the wiggly pollywog, changing in awkward stages before my eyes, becoming what it was meant to be.

When I was a child, I was sexually abused. While the abuse continued, I survived. When the abuse stopped, my recovery began. My own changing, my growth toward healing has not been a graceful "becoming," but a difficult struggle with the hard issues faced by abuse survivors. This recovery has happened in the midst of community, often with others seeing growth long before I could. I continue to move through this healing process and recognize that the scars I carry are now a part of who I am.

Secrecy and isolation, uncertainty regarding my guilt or innocence, and a basic sense of betrayal have all been a part of my experience. These experiences have affected my spirituality as they became the foundation for my understanding of myself, of others, and of God. Abuse was a central part of my earliest pictures of myself and of God. I remember my vivid childhood fear that getting close to God would destroy me. I grew up thinking that God could never love me. I grew up trying to control God, to keep God away. I grew up terrified of God.

Now, I am changing and growing and healing. The issues I face, however, are lifetime issues of learning to connect with myself, others, and the eternal, as well as searching for meaning in the midst of pain. I return to these issues as I move through new stages in my life. Abuse recovery, like spirituality, is a process. It is not measured by how far we have come, but by the journey itself.

There is freedom in acknowledging the journey. Recognizing that spiritual growth is a process, I do not have to measure myself against a list of "shoulds," or feel despair because I still struggle with issues of anger or shame or fear. All of us are on a journey, and God travels with us. There is genuine value in the journey itself, in the process of discovering all that there is to learn on the way. Acknowledging that abuse recovery is a journey, I do not have to push myself to a false and premature picture of wholeness and cover up wounds that need open air for healing. For all survivors, viewing survival as a process empowers us to continue to be honest about who we are, how we hurt, and how we are healing. As we become aware that we do not have to hide away to heal, we can know that we have something to offer to the Christian community: pictures of grace and truth that can reach beyond traditional images and challenge us to wrestle with real problems, real questions, and real pain.

My healing has meant reconstructing my image of myself, reclaiming my own sense of meaning, and reworking my relationship with God. Healing has meant letting go of guilt that isn't guilt at all. It has meant being willing to be known. I have been challenged to learn that intimacy will not mean destruction. I have taken chances by talking to God about things that I thought I could never tell anyone. My healing has meant learning to tell God what happened and talking about my fears, my joys, and my life. I have faced these challenges and taken these chances because I am convinced that the assault abused children experience creates wounds that reach as deep as the spirit, and that the healing of those wounds must reach just that deep as well.

This book is written for abuse survivors. You may be just beginning your journey. You may be feeling the depth of your wounds. You may be well along in your healing and reaching now to your soul. This is an invitation to all of us who are survivors of childhood sexual assault to reclaim our spirits and to look again at God. We can face our anger, our fears, and our losses as we experience a power that does not invade and discover a love that does not betray. We can pour out our grief and despair—even our disillusionment with God—and find one who stays with us in the journey.

Prayers provide opportunities for healing and growth. Prayer is relational. It provides an occasion for us to speak honestly about what it means to be human and to be hurt. Prayer offers relational healing. We can talk to God about the deepest concerns of our lives: our hopes and fears, our nightmares and our dreams. Therefore, prayer for survivors (as for anyone) is an exercise in personal growth and relational healing. Prayers are also reflective. They offer an opportunity for "thinking about" abuse issues in ways that can heal and transform us. Prayer can be a forum for searching for meaning, exploring questions, stating newly discovered truths, and experimenting with a different reality than that in which we have been constrained to live.

The prayers offered here address spiritual issues faced by abuse survivors. They are not solutions or answers. They are invitations to engage the questions, to present them to God and to ourselves, and to acknowledge our healing pilgrimage.

It is from my own spiritual journey and my years as a teacher, a pastor, and a counselor with abuse survivors that I have drawn the thoughts and the prayers written here. Not every prayer is about my own experience; I have also included reflections based on what others have shared with me. To all of us who are survivors of sexual assault in childhood, these prayers are offered as an invitation to spiritual healing. God stands with us as we recover from the wounds of our childhood. We can examine the ways our souls have been hurt and explore the ways our pictures of God have been shaped or misshapen by abuse. We can discover new realities about who we are and who God is. This book is an invitation to talk to God about childhood sexual abuse.

Talking to God about Abuse

What do I dare to tell you, God?
What do I dare to talk to you about?
May I speak of my anger? May I tell you of my shame? Do you
want to hear about the ugliness of the assault, of all the ways it
robbed me of my life? Do you want to know about the confusion,
the betrayal?

What do I dare to say to you, God?
What do I dare to share with you?
My disappointments?
The loneliness, the fear?
May I tell you about what he did? May I talk openly? May I be
frank? Do you want to hear about the pain of his assault? May I
tell you about the blood and the brokenness?
Do you care about the nights I can't sleep? Do you care about
the days when I struggle for the will to go on struggling?

God, what do you know about what happened? What prayers
have you answered even before I speak? Did you know about all
the times I tried to talk to others about the reality? Did you
know how I longed to share this secret? Did you know about the
pain? Do you want to know about how much I've doubted you,
how often I've hid from you, how angry I've been? Do you
remember the nights I wondered where you were? Do you
remember when you were the only one I could talk to? Do you
remember when you were the only one who listened?

What can I tell you, God? How long will you listen? Will you
stay with me until I grow tired of telling? Until the sting is taken
out of the words?
Until the power is taken out of the memory?
Will you stay with me until my healing comes?

God, I want to talk to you about childhood sexual abuse.
God, I want to tell you about my abuse.
God who listens, listen to me.

Moving toward Wholeness

Child sexual abuse wounds its victims deeply. Some of the wounds can be seen. The blood, the bruises, the torn bodies tell us of the physical pain. Other injuries are not as easily detected. Suggestive glances, furtive touching, and words whispered in secret may not leave physical scars. But all abuse leaves wounds: a child's sense of self is crushed, a soaring spirit is held down and hurt, a capacity to trust is taken away and replaced by shame and guilt. To see these injuries, we must look closer. These invisible wounds and scars reach a survivor's soul.

Being sexually assaulted as a child is devastating. At the core of the experience are pain and betrayal. Someone with power over us—parent, relative, older sibling, babysitter, church leader, neighbor, or stranger—used that power to hurt and humiliate. Someone who should have cared for us injured us instead, exploited our innocence, took advantage of our weakness. And then the abuser often found a way to keep us silent about the experience. Explicit or implicit threats, statements about "our" guilt, confusing messages about what was happening are ways we may have been manipulated. When we couldn't tell anyone what was happening, we grew up with secrets that kept us separate from all around us. Sometimes our secrets kept us separate even from ourselves. The brokenness that arises out of the betrayal, the secrecy, the fear, and the confusion of sexual assault touches the heart of our spiritual journey.

At the heart of spirituality are two equally important dimensions. Spirituality can first be described as connectedness. This includes connections with ourselves, with others, and with the eternal—the outward journey. Spirituality can also be described as our human search for meaning in existence. This second dimension focuses on a more inward journey. As we understand our separateness and individuality, we discover that a sense of our own significance comes from our unique life experiences. This dual drive toward connectedness and purpose is what fuels our journey to wholeness. Both of these aspects of spirituality include skills that human beings develop and practice throughout life. From birth, we separate and connect over and over again. These two dimensions of spirituality give life balance. And for those of us who are abuse survivors, each of these realities, our connectedness and our sense of meaning, has been affected by the assaults we experienced as children.

We are all born as dependent beings. That dependency at first makes us quite vulnerable. From the beginning of our existence, we strive to make connections. We must learn to be in relationship. And if in our vulnerable state we are cared for, protected, and loved, we experience the spirituality of connectedness. For all people, this link between dependency and personal vulnerability has tremendous implications for spiritual as well as personal development. To learn to be in relationship, we need to be open to self, others, and God. For abuse survivors, however, betrayal by those who were responsible for our care and the exploitation of our vulnerability leads to a genuine struggle with dependency. As children, we experienced that those with power in our lives used that power in ways that crushed our spirits of connectedness. Our vulnerability did not lead to the connecting experience of care and love, but to the shattering experience of betrayal and fear.

As a result of childhood abuse, we struggle with fear any time we become vulnerable to another person or experience power in a relationship. When power has been used to damage rather than to care for, power becomes a scary thing. When being known has meant being hurt, openness becomes scary. And we bring each of these struggles to our relationship with ourselves, with others, and with God. As human beings, we long to be known, to be valued, to be cherished. As abuse survivors, we struggle with our terror of being "found out," used, and abandoned. We struggle with fear or shame any time someone comes near enough to begin to know us.

Our connecting task includes learning how we connect with or are alienated from ourselves as well. The injuries of childhood sexual abuse can touch every level of our sense of self. In our healing, each of these parts of ourselves and of our spirituality can be reclaimed. Our spirit, as the integration point for our bodies, our feelings, and our ways of thinking about ourselves, as well as our relationships and our personal choices, can heal the fragmentation that abuse causes. In our spirits we can reconnect with ourselves.

There are five levels on which we can connect with ourselves. First, on the most basic level of existence, we are physical beings. Our bodies are a central part of our sense of self. When we were abused, the integrity of our connection with our bodies was challenged and the vulnerability of our bodies was exploited. Many of us feel that our bodies betrayed us. Our survival may have included developing the ability to dissociate, or literally emotionally separate ourselves from, what was happening to us physically. Feelings about sexuality and love have been distorted by assault, and our connections with our own sexuality may have been affected. The physical and the spiritual are connected. Exploring spirituality and child sexual abuse will include an invitation to reconciliation with our physical self. We can live in our bodies. We can embrace and celebrate our sexuality. We can become whole.

Sexual abuse also affects our feelings and our ways of thinking about our world. As we heal, we are called to reconnect with the emotional and the cognitive components of our sense of self.

A second level of connection is emotional. Our emotional healing will include dealing with all the feelings we have had about our abuse. As adults in recovery, we may be surprised by the intensity of our feelings, still fresh after so many years. How can such feelings be a part of our spirituality? Throughout the history of the church, people have wondered about the "acceptability" of certain emotions. The spiritual person has been presented as one who is not affected by feelings or does not respond to situations with the same emotional intensity as others. Some have even defined spirituality as the absence of emotion. It is important to challenge any image of spirituality that rejects all or even some feelings, and to embrace emotion as a part of what it means to be human. The emotions we experienced as abused children, including fear, terror, pain, and outrage, will be a part of our spirituality. The whole range of human feelings can be embraced by our healing spirit.

Cognitive issues are a third part of survivor spirituality. Questions and doubts fill our minds. How are these very real doubts to be reconciled with faith? We struggle with questions about the abuse: Why did my uncle do that? Why did God let that happen? Those questions can pound in the mind and tear at the soul. For many of us, such questions and doubts have been significant blocks to a connection with God. We have felt the need either to reject our thoughts or to reject God. In working toward spiritual growth, it is helpful to know that doubts are a part of faith. Questions that may never be answered can still be asked. What a delight to discover that God does not demand unquestioning belief, but rather stands with us in the times of doubting too.

The fourth aspect of our connectedness is relational. Our abuse has affected more than our connections with our bodies and with our feelings and our thinking about our world. It has affected our relational self as well. While children typically reach out to others and learn basic lessons of mutuality, as abused children we learned not to connect with others, but to protect ourselves. All the dynamics of relationships, elements of separateness and connection, giving and taking, self-sufficiency and interdependence have been skewed by the abuse. Secrecy has kept us isolated. In our healing, we can experience the personal growth and spiritual growth that includes exploring and developing basic relationship skills of trust, openness, care, and love.

Finally, our sense of our personal integrity may have been affected by abuse. Many of us carry a tremendous amount of guilt, imagining we somehow caused our abuse. We have difficulty acknowledging that we were not responsible for what happened to us. If we disclosed the abuse, we struggle to understand that we were not responsible for what may have happened to our abuser. Maya Angelou, in describing her childhood rape, talks about her sense of guilt and responsibility when her rapist was killed: "Obviously, I had forfeited my place in heaven forever. . . . Even Christ had turned his back on Satan. Wouldn't He turn His back on me? I could feel the evilness flowing through my body and waiting, pent up, to rush off my tongue if I tried to open my mouth."[1]

A basic, intense, significant relationship between guilt, control, and trust existed in our lives as abused children. This relationship defined our reality then and profoundly affects our spirituality now. We lived in a world we could not trust, perhaps even a world of terror. We found that for relief we had to be in control, find some way to regulate our out-of-control world. We found reassurance in our myth that we were somehow in charge: "I can make this abuse stop if I just try hard enough. I can make them love me." This false sense of control permitted our psychological survival.

The trade-off for the relief from the constant terror, the constant threat, was guilt. This awful guilt, the sense that "I caused my abuse" or "I was abused because of something that is wrong with me," is common to most of us. We decided it was better to feel responsible than to feel vulnerable. Better to feel "in charge" than to realize the truth, that there was nothing we could do to stop the powerful adult. Abuse is *never* the child's fault, but that is hard for children to believe, because hopelessness and helplessness are much more frightening than guilt. Learning to let go of guilt is a therapeutic issue. It is also a central issue in spiritual healing.

Some of us may have also turned our trauma outward and acted out in ways that genuinely hurt others. What are the moral issues involved, for example, when a child, hurt by adults, turns around and hurts other children? Where does responsibility rest when a young girl, sexually assaulted by a family member, begins to use sex as a way of relating to all men and becomes pregnant at age sixteen? For some of us, issues of chemical dependency arise because alcohol and drugs are used to dull the pain.

What choices have we made in our reactions to our abuse? How do we as abuse survivors begin to take responsibility for and become accountable for personal choices? Because issues of guilt and responsibility are so often confused in the mind of a young child, moral struggles and confusion may be a significant part of our spiritual questioning, as well. In connecting with ourselves, looking honestly at our own choices and responsibilities as adults is a part of the challenge of personal and spiritual growth.

These components of human personality—physical, emotional, mental, relational, and ethical—are significant aspects of our connections with ourselves. Each of these aspects of ourselves may give important clues to our spirituality; each may at different times in life be a key issue. Spirituality, however, is more than any of these parts of the self. Spirituality gives each of these parts direction and meaning, and brings each together into a whole. Healing from childhood abuse means healing each of these parts. Spiritual recovery embraces each, as well, and offers the opportunity for wholeness.

The second dimension of spirituality takes us beyond connectedness to individuation. In our spiritual journey each of us needs to find personal meaning and significance. Beyond our connectedness is an individual autonomy that allows us to experience spiritual strength even when connections are broken or not available. Our autonomy is reflected in our power to choose. We can exercise this power and find a sense of purpose and significance that can help us survive and grow in even the harshest of places.

As a survivor of a German concentration camp, Victor Frankl observed the close relationship between spirituality, personhood, and choice when he explored the human search for meaning in that horror-filled setting.[2] In the death camp, he observed that having a sense of purpose and discovering personal significance, even in the midst of despair, were key factors in prisoners' capacity to survive. An individual's ability to acquire perspective and some sense of meaning even in the midst of intolerable living conditions can mean the difference between life and death.

As sexual abuse survivors, we have also lived through intolerable experiences. The task of finding personal meaning and personal faith in the face of these experiences is a central challenge of our spirituality. As survivors of childhood sexual abuse, we join all people of faith who have struggled to connect with God in the midst of suffering and evil. The words of many of the Psalms, of Lamentations and Jeremiah, and of Job demonstrate the power of speaking to God about betrayal, pain, and anger. Those victims of oppression and injustice did not remain silent. They openly struggled with their questions and their rage at all who were a part of such evil. They even argued with God. Out of their struggles, they offer us a tradition of God's willingness to listen to our anger, doubts, pain, and even vengeful hate. God is capable of hearing all that we have to say.

Our whole self, then, is called to healing. All parts of ourselves are called to reconciliation, to the discovery of a sense of oneness, to integrity, to connection. Our whole self is also called to discover meaning and purpose in our existence, even in the midst of suffering. God welcomes all of who we are, in our physical pain and alienation, in our confusion and questions, in our fears and rage, in our loneliness and isolation, in our struggles with questions of responsibility, guilt, and shame. Discovering that welcome connection and empowering significance is neither simple nor easy. Spiritual growth may come slowly and is always a process, rather than a finished product. In their workbook for survivors, *The Courage to Heal*, Ellen Bass and Laura Davis emphasize that "spirituality is not a shortcut through any of the stages of healing."[3] As we begin to take risks, we learn new truths and new ways of being. Lessons in connecting and in separating that were unavailable to us as abused children can be claimed by us now as adult survivors.

As we begin to claim our new wholeness, we also learn to break the silence regarding sexual abuse. Marie Fortune explores the impact of silence in her book *Sexual Violence, The Unmentionable Sin*. She tells us all that "silence begets silence. The tightness of the circle is overwhelming at times."[4] When we begin to speak as survivors, we break out of that tight, silent circle. Speaking means more than telling someone about the abuse, although that is an important and often very difficult step. Breaking silence can also mean talking about the reality of what life is like for us.

There are many ways of talking about abuse: growing beyond a mentality that might seek to qualify or quantify abuse, refusing to assume that one type of traumatic assault might be more or less damaging than another, moving out of denial and minimization and into an acknowledgment that all levels of childhood assault are betrayals, speaking about our pain with a clarity that others may not want to hear. And there are ways of breaking the internal silence: remembering long-forgotten events, which memory set aside for the sake of our psychological survival, acknowledging the depth of our injuries, facing the abuse on a level that we may not want to face, learning to listen to ourselves.

Breaking the silence can mean beginning to talk to God about our abuse as well. For some of us this can be a starting point for healing. For others this step will come as we are well into our recovery. As wounded children we learned to conceal the levels of pain and loss from family and friends because we were told to, or because we feared the truth would not be believed, or because it seemed too overwhelming. Many of us have learned also to "hide" from God. Talking to God about our childhood sexual abuse means placing before God all the fears, the rage, and the confusion of the hurting child. Breaking silence with God may mean standing before God and asking why. It may mean ending a pattern of "taking care" of God, trying to put a nice face on the raw pain, or ending every prayer with a "happily ever after" in an attempt to keep God happy. We may have had a tendency to say, "Well, yes, it was hard, but everything's OK now, so please don't leave me." Breaking silence with God means telling God the truth.

For those who doubt that God is or that God is listening, breaking silence on a spiritual level can have a profound impact on personal recovery. To acknowlede abuse and examine the ways it has shaped our sense of self, our personal understanding of the meaning and purpose of our lives, and our relationship to a reality beyond ourselves is a spiritual exercise. Speaking the truth about this, out loud to the universe, can empower the soul. Even telling God about our doubts is a freeing exercise. Doubts do not disqualify us from spiritual growth. The doubts themselves, and a willingness to express them, are often significant signs of growth.

This process of talking to God opens up to us the two dimensions of spiritual growth I have been discussing. In talking, we can find honest connectedness. In talking, in telling our stories, we can find our own significance and purpose and meaning. We can hear the power of survival and of refusing to be conquered by evil. In being heard, we can find honest connectedness. We hear ourselves and discover wholeness within. Others hear, and we create community. God listens, and we discover a bond with the eternal.

Our healing touches all of who we are. Our speaking touches all whom our lives touch. Ellen Bass and Laura Davis say this: "A healing spirituality is . . . a passion for life, a feeling of connection, of being a part of the life around you."[5] In our journey, as we talk, as we pray, we can find connectedness and significance and healing for our spirits as well.

Approaching the Pain

When I was small the words would not come.
I could not speak.
The people looked at me and asked about me
    and wondered about me,
but I couldn't speak.
I was silent, and they shook their heads and walked away.

Now I am grown, and words come.
I speak.
The people look at me and ask about me
    and wonder about me still,
and I speak.
I say, "Yes, children do get hurt." I say, "No, I don't understand."
I say, "child sexual abuse." I say, "incest." I say, "pain."
Then they look beyond me and long to be gone,
    away from my painful truths.
They shake their heads and walk away.

But you, Jesus, you tell stories of people who listened.
You tell stories of those who stopped and stooped
    to hear the pain.
Samaritans, approaching the wounded.
Willing to feel pain as they listen to pain.
You tell stories of seeing, of hearing, of neighbors, of love.

And you, Jesus. You say, "Tell me."
You say, "Speak. I am not afraid to feel."
You approach the pain.
You teach me that pain will not destroy.
When the storm is over, the resurrection begins.

Amen.

The Weaver

I celebrate a mother God,
gently weaving, working carefully.
I celebrate the hands of skill, creating beauty within me.
I celebrate the working of the loom, reconnecting myself,
weaving a tapestry that picks up threads of pain and anger and
grief and loss, and power and courage and strength and grace.

Here are the broken threads. This should have been solid here.
This innocence should have continued on, this openness should
have come through here, this pattern of trust should have been
right here, making a design that all would see
and say, "What beauty!"
But these threads were broken, ripped from the fabric of me, and
I was afraid to show anyone the tear.
I thought it was my fault, that all would look
and say, "What horror!"
Now we pick up this broken thread, my weaving God and me.
Now we do the work of repair, and as the fabric is made strong
I look in surprise and say to myself, "What beauty I reclaim!"
Out of the torn places, I reclaim wholeness.
Out of the broken places, I reclaim strength.
Out of the shatteredness, I reclaim power.
Out of the horror and the shame and the pain, I reclaim
openness, innocence, courage.

The Weaver will not be discouraged or deterred.
We weave a fabric which no one's violence will destroy,
and I discover the beauty of me.

Amen.

That Day He Touched Me

That day he touched me I wasn't doing anything wrong.
I thought he loved me. I thought I was safe.
It was just a day, like a normal day, just a day and then
everything was changed.

My God,
How can I explain to you the relaxed way we were together?
My feet bare, swinging in the water,
sitting beside him because I loved him,
leaning into his warm grown-up body,
feeling his arm around my shoulder, feeling the safety
and the joy and
then it changed.
His hand moved. My body froze. My mind froze.
My smile, my warm smile, froze.

My God,
how can I explain to you the shattering of that day?
No safety.
No joy.
Only frozen fear and pain.

That day he touched me I wasn't doing anything wrong.
Why did he take it all away from me?

My Journey

My journey is from brokenness to wholeness.
The breaking happened a long time ago when I was just a child.
Body torn from me. Feelings torn mind torn choices torn.
People torn from me.

I was left to pick up the pieces, to put myself back together again.
My little child hands were not graceful or gifted, but I did the
patching the best I could, and I continued on.
I grew.

I found on my journey that the brittle shell my childhood hands
had made could no longer contain all that was me.
It could not bend with my stretching, it could not shift with my
own fierce healing, so
I broke through.

My journey is from brokenness to wholeness. With these strong
scars my body knitted to my heart to my mind to my soul, and
I became free to stretch my wings at last.
I flew.

The Language of Truth

What is the language spoken here?
This is the language of truth.
To say what really happened, to talk about how I really feel.
No veiled references, no covered up words,
but to say this happened, this happened; to tell myself the truth.
What is the language spoken here?
I hear the words of truth.
True emotion, anger, loss.
He hurt me, she left me.
They were too scared, they scared me.
I look for a place where I can hear the words of my native tongue.
I have been a stranger in their midst too long.
Now I speak the language of truth.
The choking in my throat screams truth.
The aching in my soul insists on truth.
Now I speak my native tongue.
Here I tell the truth.

Amen.

Anger

God, I work to direct my anger where it belongs.
Not at me, an innocent child,
but at the one who stole my innocence.
God, this anger spills into so many areas of my life.
Sometimes it hits only the safest targets.
Me, or the people I love,
or you.

God, it is so hard to put this anger where it belongs,
the place that feels unsafest of all.

God help me direct my anger where it belongs,
and then let its white heat purify me
and let its truth redeem me
and let its justice transform me
that I may be renewed and that I may be set free.

Amen.

Grief

Comforter of those who mourn,
I stand before you as one in mourning.
Because of innocence lost, trust that was stolen,
    sexuality distorted,
I grieve.
Because of a childhood of no exploring, no wondering,
    no sweet curiosity,
I mourn.
Because of adolescence with no gradual unfolding,
    no gentle discovering, no choices of whom I will love,
I grieve.
Because of adulthood gained from loss, from pain,
    from struggle,
I mourn.
I stand before you as one who grieves.
Stand with me as I recognize the anguish of my loss.

Amen.

Night Prayer

Now I lay me down to sleep,
> *his hand moves under the sheet*
> *his hand moves on my body*
> *"Don't do that," I whisper, to one who doesn't hear.*

I pray the Lord my soul to keep,
> *Please keep my soul, please keep my soul*
> *This body I don't want to keep*
> *This body I don't want to feel*
> *"Please don't do that."*

If I should die before I wake,
> *Will I die before I wake?*
> *Will his visits kill me?*
> *Will the death leak through?*
> *Will this pain that cuts so deeply*
> *This pain that I refuse to feel*
> *Will this kill me?*

I pray the Lord my soul to take.
> *God, will you really take me?*
> *Will you really love me?*
> *Will you hurt me?*
> *Please don't let me feel his touch*
> *Please don't hurt me*
> *Please don't hate me*
> *Please.*

In Jesus' name I pray, amen.

Body Talk

God of incarnation, Word become flesh,
It is so hard for me to talk to you about my body.
I long to reconnect with what was stolen from me.
I search for a way to separate sexual assault from sexuality, and
to rediscover the beauty of your gift of the physical.
So many times my body has felt like a trap, like evil, like pain.
My body scares me and I'm scared to tell you that. To survive
I had to disconnect, to deny, to learn to feel nothing.
Now, in healing, in growing, I discover my desire to reconnect,
to learn new lessons about this physical me.
To find a home here in this body, which I so quickly left when it
was being hurt, when it was being assaulted.
To know the joy of giving, not the terror of being robbed.
To know the pleasure of physical love.
To find a home in me.
These are the longings I feel in my flesh.
Word become flesh, God of incarnation,
lead me to the healing of this body,
to the reconnection of body and spirit,
to the place of wholeness in myself.

Amen.

Just Talking

God, I just want to talk to you. I just want to open my soul to you. I don't want to try to say it right. I don't want to meet someone else's expectations of what I should say or what I should believe.
I just want to talk to you.

I sit sometimes in a deep well. I can't get out. I'm so tired of the struggle. I ache. I want to stop time and spend time with me. But time moves on and takes me with it.

God, I'm too tired to hold on, and I don't know any way out. This aching human part of me, what do I do with this?
God, you have abandoned me. I cannot pretend that I feel you here. I cannot pretend that I'm OK. All I can do is hold on and hope this feeling will pass. All I can do is trust that it will stop and when I pass through, you will be there on the other side.

Amen.

Rest Here

Sad today. Very sad.
The sadness seeps out through my eyes.
My throat chokes.
Too sad to look up.
Too sad to reach out.
I need a god who reaches me beyond, in spite of, sadness.
I need you to invite me:
"Rest here,"
I want to hear you say.
"Rest here and know that you are safe."

Safe? What does that mean? How can that be?
The sadness cuts me, and you say that I can be safe.

Safe in my sadness.
Safe from looks that sting and words that sting
        and hands that sting.
Safe from the all-encompassing fear.
"Rest here."

Is there healing?
Will you stay with me?
I speak, I pray to pour out my heart, my soul,
to scream into the silence,
to hear the echo of silence back to me.
First the scream,
then the silence.
Where are you, God?

Do You Care?

My Friend who keeps listening through all the pain,
I needed to reach out and tell you how hard things seem to be in
this healing work I'm doing. I wish there were words to explain
the shock, the terror, the trembling that overwhelms me. Inside
I grow small. Outside I grow quiet. Why do people have to hurt?
Why do people have to hurt babies?
Do you care?

The inside shattering leaves me wondering if I will ever be whole.
The inside wounding leaves me wondering if the looking will
always bring pain. Slivers from my splintered soul run deep into
my own hands when I try to explore the truth, when I try to
reach for wholeness. What does it mean to be crushed so young?
Broken by the indifference and pain and anger of a big person
who thought he needed my body more than I did.
Can I afford to care for me?

Friend who listens to all my anger,
I used to pray all the time. Now I can barely talk to you. Now I
look for release and find nothing but a vague hope within me
that refuses to die. When my fists tried to shatter walls the way
another's fists broke me, I searched for release. When my
knuckles bled and reminded me of the childhood blood, I was
seeking peace.
Do you care?

Now I'm finding my way. Your love does not take the pain away;
your love does not banish the anger. Your love stands with me
through the pain, through the anger, and listening Friend,
I can learn to care.

Amen.

Remembering

God, help me to remember now.
No, don't.
God, I'm ready to see the pictures now.
Wait stop.
OK. That's OK. I just needed to catch my breath. Now I'm ready.
Please don't let me see.
There. Just resting for a minute. Now you can start.
Wait. I'm sorry. I'm not ready yet.
God, I have to see. I want to see, I want to know the truth,
and let the truth set me free. I'm strong enough now.
Please let me begin now.
No, not that truth. God, that's too close, it hurts too much.
Please let me look.
Please don't make me look.

God, please just hold me. I'm so tired. Please just let me rest.
The pictures
memories at the edges of my mind knocking on the door:
"Let me in let me in,"
waiting for me, waiting patient.

"When you're ready you will see. Know I hold you safe until then.
Know I walk with you when you start to walk.
Know I run without growing tired
alongside you as you run from or run to.
Know that I am God your Mother who carries you
God your Father who lifts you
not to hit you not to hurt you not to tell you no
but yes yes yes.
Yes, I love you."

Amen.

A Refuge

My Refuge,
I get so scared so scared.
So scared of . . .
people who hurt others
people who are mean
memories that overwhelm
emptiness
fullness
You.

Scared of failure,
scared of rejection,
scared of "wrong, wrong, wrong."
Scared of all these feelings inside me that leave me
small and shaking.
Scared of pain.
You say, "Perfect love casts out fear."
My Refuge, I'm afraid to ask you:
Bring your perfect love to me.

Amen.

Hope

It seemed to me, God, that you left when I needed you.
When I cried out, the silence only
magnified the echoes of my cry.
No answer. No answer. No deliverance.
When I was little I asked for favors:
Don't let the kitten die. Don't let my grandma die.
But you didn't grant favors.
When I grew bigger, they told me just to trust.
God answers prayer.
You just have to trust. Stories of people finding parking places,
or selling homes, or getting work when they asked for your help.
Then where were you those nights he came into my room?
When he invaded my soul while invading my body?
Where were you when he took me in the shower,
making me dirty
while pretending to make me clean?
Now I ask no favors.
Now I do not trust.
Now I know nothing about how or why to pray.
Now I know I only turn to you, and hold on somehow, and hope.

Amen.

Evils Done in Your Name

This is a prayer for memories, God, of evils done in your name.
I know that wasn't really you,
    but how's a child supposed to know?
And when I bow in prayer now,
    what do I do with the memories of pain?
And when I turn to you now,
    what do I do with the fear?
My fear, my childhood training, that tells me you were on his side?
That bad girls go to hell? That your anger is swift and thorough,
    and poured out on such a one as me?

This is a prayer for healing, God, of evils done in your name.
Now it is time to learn who you are. I will no longer accept
those pictures I was given, those images I was taught to fear.
I will no longer accept the anger and the pain and the terror
given to me in your name.
Now I want to learn your name, now I want to see you new.
I bring myself to you today, God,
    and trust to find a gentle touch.

Amen.

Hard to Remember

Gentle Parent, keeper of memories,
You know how easily I forget.
In angry hard times I forget about the peaceful times.
In scary trembling times I forget about the safe times.
I need your help to remember.

When shame and doubt have captured me,
remind me of my innocence and your faithfulness.
When loneliness convinces me that I have been abandoned,
remind me of my strength and your presence.
When the despair of slow recovery seems to block my path
        to wholeness,
remind me that I can go on, and that you give food
        for the journey.
Lead me today in the way I have chosen
        (though I sometimes forget),
the way of healing and love.

Amen.

Coming Back to Myself

Great Healer, I had hoped the wound wouldn't be this deep.
I didn't know when he hurt me that I was so shattered.
My Comforter, I had hoped the pain wouldn't last this long.
When I felt it first, I thought I could stop it.
Gentle Healer, I had hoped that the healing wouldn't be so slow.
I wanted to be over it and through it and on with my life.

Now I'm learning how much a child is hurt with this hurting.
Now I feel the depth of pain I had to deny for so long.
Now I know the slow slow process of recovery,
of picking up the pieces,
of coming back to myself.

Amen.

Prayer for Tenderness

Creator of love, of tenderness, of quiet and of gentleness,
my healing soul reaches out to you as a young child reaching
    for mother, for nurture, for care.
When I was young I was taught not to reach.
My arms just folded across myself, seeking safety when safety
    could not be found.
Creator, you know that most of the time I still hold on
    to my isolation,
mistaking it for strength.
I hold on to my tears, and they do not escape except when words
    of tenderness catch me off guard and speak to my soul.
Then, my Creator, I reach for you, for love and tenderness
    and gentleness and mother. Hold me and heal me.

Amen.

To Trust Again

As I learn to trust again, there is so much to learn.

God, I'm learning to trust myself. What a surprise, that there is so much inside of me to learn to trust. I'm learning to listen to me inside, to pay attention, to really hear.
I'm learning about my own wisdom, that I do know what is at the heart of me, what I want, what I feel, what I need.

God, I'm learning to trust other people. There are people in this world who do what they say they will do. I'm learning to sort through people. I'm learning the difference between those who have hurt me and those who have not. I'm learning, gingerly, carefully, to put my weight down full on that which can hold me up.

God, I'm learning to trust you. I'm learning to put into words things I have been afraid to tell you. I'm learning that your steadfast love endures forever, that you will not abandon me, that you do not lie to me. I'm learning that you do not hurt me, call me stupid, run out of patience, forget to do what you said you would, change your mind, change the rules.

God, I'm learning to trust the truth. I'm learning its power, its freedom.
I'm learning that I can speak truth, believe truth, believe me.

Amen.

God Who Walks with Us

When Celie, the main character in Alice Walker's novel *The Color Purple*, is raped by her stepfather, he warns her to tell no one but God.[1] Throughout her childhood, Celie follows that order, and so it is to God that she pours out her heart, asks her questions, and offers her reflections on life. Much of this powerful novel takes the form of Celie's dialogue with God, and her growing and changing experience of who God is and who she is.

Turning to God when all other sources for help have been forbidden is not unusual for those of us who are survivors of childhood sexual abuse. With no one else to speak to as children, some of us spoke to God and found a connection that empowered us, a sense of hope and purpose in our hopeless world. Those of us with this experience value the spiritual connection we were able to find as children and have continued to develop a powerful relationship with God as adults. We have known some of our only feelings of safety, comfort, and value in the presence of God.

For others of us, however, God's place in our world has not always been comforting or clear. We called out for help and no one came. We cried out for relief and felt only more pain. We felt abandoned and alone, isolated from God's care, and perhaps even rejected by God. Some of us were even told or came to believe that God somehow was responsible for the abuse. We may have felt singled out by God for punishment. We felt the need to hide from God. There were moments, perhaps, when we gave up on God.

Still others of us have had both these experiences with God. We have known times of feeling connected to God and of sensing God's presence when we needed a friend. But we also knew times when the silence of the heavens seemed to confirm our deepest fears that even God could not or would not hear our cries. These experiences touch our spirituality because at their heart they speak to our connectedness to the eternal and to our own search for meaning and significance.

As I discussed earlier, many abuse survivor issues center on relationships. Our earliest experiences in relationships were fear, pain, abandonment, and betrayal. To each new relationship we bring our struggles with trust, control, and shame. These are also the issues we bring to God. The opportunity to explore our image of God and our relationship with God is therefore also an opportunity for personal and spiritual healing.

It is often said that our basic image of God is formed by the time we are three years old. Everything after that is simply refinement. At a very young age, we make foundational decisions about who we are, why we exist, and how we relate to whatever is beyond us. We are, every one of us as children, young theologians. David Heller reported his research on children's images of God in the article "The Children's God." He observed: "All of the children I studied seemed to weave their most pressing emotional concerns into the fabric of their God."[2]

Russell Baker provides a compelling example of that process when he writes in *Growing Up* about his early experiences with "God pictures," conclusions he came to when his father died of complications from alcoholism and diabetes. Baker was only five years old at the time and reports that for the first time he began to think about God. He remembers: "Between sobs, I told Bessie that if God could do things like this to people, then God was hateful and I had no use for Him." This experience with childhood trauma led Baker to conclude that "God was a lot less interested in people than anybody in Morrisonville was willing to admit."[3] Baker experienced childhood trauma, and his view of God was profoundly affected.

The most pressing emotional concerns that we as abuse survivors weave into our understanding of God focus on basic psychological survival. When boundaries are violated so young, our very sense of self is affected. Difficult personal tasks such as discovering and defining ourselves, learning to relax in relationships, learning to give of ourselves in a free and genuine way are all foundational to spirituality, and they are all made more difficult by the betrayal inflicted by abuse.

For many, in addition, our abuse is actually linked to God in some way. Those of us who were also physically abused may have been told that "God approves" of this sort of "discipline." Those of us who prayed for help and relief from an intolerable situation often found no answers to our prayers. Concepts such as "love" and "forgiveness" may have been misapplied in ways that have since tortured our souls. At times God may have even been brought directly into the abuse situation.

I remember hearing a man talk to a group of people about abusing his son. He described how he would begin a "playful wrestling match" with the young boy, which would end in sexual assault. He then told us what would happen next: "My son and I would get down on our knees and ask for God's forgiveness. We would pray that God would help us not to do that again."

I was stunned. What went through the mind of that little boy, kneeling there in pain and confusion and fear? What was that young child's view of God—and of himself? First, his father implied in the "prayer time" that the boy shared the guilt, that he was not a victim but a willing participant. According to dad, God had to "forgive" this young child. Then, each time the boy was molested again, he had to conclude that for some reason God had not answered their prayer, had not helped it to "not happen again." He was being taught, in a painful way, from a warped perspective: God's back is turned to the cries of an abused child.

As adult survivors, we can look again at our pictures of God. Our images of God, formed at times when fear and pain dominated our emotional landscape, can be reformed. For some of us, that may mean moving away from traditional but inadequate views of God or from painful images of "father." For some of us, healing may include connecting with female images of the Reality beyond ourselves. There are powerful images of God as Healer, or Light, or Pioneer that can move us toward wholeness. In *The Courage to Heal*, Ellen Bass and Laura Davis have observed this: "Whether you have a fixed concept of God, believe there is a life spirit coursing through us all, or simply trust your own intuition, having faith in something more powerful and constant than your shifting emotions and ideas can be a great comfort to you as you heal." [4]

Those of us who had to learn not to be vulnerable can discover Gentleness. Those of us who learned to fear power can discover Empowerment. Those of us who learned to shape our reality to fit others' demands can discover the freedom of Truth.

We do, of course, face hard questions about God as we form a sense of personal significance in the face of personal suffering. Where is God when innocent people suffer? Where is God when children are being hurt? Where is God when we wander through our own wilderness of pain and fear? These questions are an important part of our relationship with God. Simplistic answers about how God answers prayer do not suffice to explain childhood sexual abuse. The truth is that the abuse happened whether we prayed for it to stop or not. Where was God?

Such questions regarding the power of evil and the presence of God are not new. They have challenged individuals throughout time. When we look boldly at the reality of pain and suffering in our world, simple answers cannot be found. God does not stop abuse. God does not stop suffering. That is not the way God works in our world. God has given human beings freedom that can lead to profound personal meaning. But the other side of this freedom offers the possibility of profound evil. There is tremendous value to this freedom and there is also tremendous cost.

In the same way we make choices about our own purpose and meaning, even in the presence of horror, we also make choices about our pictures of God. It is an affirmation of faith to say that God does not abandon us in the midst of suffering. God may not have stopped the abuse, but God does stand with us and weep with us in every difficult place. Our pain and rage are real, and God feels that pain and rage with us. God is with us even when we walk through the valley of the shadow of death. The journey is still ours to take, but we do not take it alone.

As abuse survivors, we are not only reforming our image of God, we are also redeveloping our relationship with God. This too presents challenges. We are learning to trust, and we are learning to be vulnerable. We are reworking our understanding of power as a relationship dynamic.

My own experience of connections with others has always seemed tentative. What can it mean to be accepted unconditionally? Yes, I know you've said you like me, but what if you really *knew* me? What if you knew the struggles, the despair, the anger and hate I sometimes feel? Every time you tell me something good you see in me, I counter it with a hundred negatives, and once again feel alone. And so your acceptance is comforting, but I wonder if it can stand up to truth. And if our relationship cannot handle "truth," do we have a relationship at all? These fears also were transferred to my connection with God.

As abused children we were trained not to value truth. We could not tell the truth to our abusers without risking even greater pain than we were already enduring. We were warned against telling the truth to others. We built relationships while keeping a secret and thus found that no matter how close we got to someone, there was always a distance that had to be maintained. Some of us who did try to tell the truth met with doubt and denial. Even as adults we may have been told, It wasn't that bad, or That's in the past. Why don't you move on? Our inability to speak the truth, or the inability of others to hear it, was always separating us from them. And if you do know me, then what? If there is truth in our friendship, can you still be my friend? Can grace and truth really stand together?

The writer of the Gospel of John describes God as God is seen in Jesus. In Jesus that writer had discovered "truth and grace." This provides a model for relating to God that can begin to reach abuse survivors. It has been an empowering model for me.

The story of Jesus and the Samaritan woman is recorded in John 4. That story illustrates the possibilities in joining truth and grace; in the discovery that we can tell the truth about ourselves and still find acceptance. Jesus meets a woman outside her city in Samaria. In the course of their conversation, he offers the woman a gift—living water—from a well that will never run dry. Yet when the woman asks to receive the gift, she is told, "Go call your husband." This presents a dilemma: the woman hesitates to tell Jesus the truth about her life. She answers, "I have no husband." Jesus acknowledges that her statement is correct and then goes on to tell her that he already knows her story: "You have had five husbands, and the man you are living with now is not your husband."

What an intriguing encounter. Perhaps the woman was thinking, This man speaks as a spiritual person. Would he be so willing to speak to me if he really knew me? In this story, that concern is addressed when Jesus brings up questions about the woman's husband. In telling her that he already knows her, Jesus is also saying, I've offered you this gift with the full knowledge of who you are. I know you *and* I love you. By the time the conversation is over, the woman is running back to town, calling out, "Come see a man who told me everything I ever did. Could this be the Messiah?" This woman's reality, which had been a source of isolation and shame, is now proclaimed as good news. Truth is merged with grace. Here she has found one who who can tell her everything she has ever done and who loves her still.

This story identifies our dilemma in relationships: Our shame and fear set up a wall through which nothing can pass. For every gift, every warm compliment, every kind connection offered, we have our own answer: If you really knew me, this gift would not have been offered. If you knew me, you would stay away.

However, the reality about God that we as abuse survivors can experience is this: God knows us already—knows our fears, our pain, our innocence, and our mistakes. God's offer of relationship does not depend on our ability to earn it, to do or say the "right" thing, or to somehow make ourselves worthy. God knows us, and God loves us. This is perfect love, full of truth and grace. This is love that casts out fear.[5]

In naming God as one who is full of both truth and grace, we discover the foundation for a full relationship with God. All that we are can be known. All that we are can be loved. God does not insist that we make the picture better or cover up our deepest fears, doubts, or feelings of guilt. God invites truth in the presence of grace and thus provides the foundation for true relationship. Our pain, our shame, our secrets—all are welcomed here. We do not need to control this relationship to survive.

The task of coming to terms with our image of God may not be an easy one for abuse survivors. As people who are used to hiding, trying to stay safe, living alone or unconnected, to change this established pattern of relating can be difficult. Many of us have spent years trying to control God. But the effort to be always in control is exhausting and alienating. We survivors, we who have learned not to reach out, how do we now begin to reach out to God? This is the challenge and the opportunity offered here. It may be slow, tedious, and frustrating, as well as frightening, to try new connections. It may take great effort to rethink our understanding of God. However, it is possible. It can even be empowering. Acknowledging the fear and validating the genuineness of our felt need for control are initial steps.

There is nothing we need to do—or even can do—to earn God's love. Love is simply present in the relationship. This may be a completely foreign concept to those of us who grew up desperately trying to learn how to control our abusers. It may take time and effort to incorporate "honesty" into our relationship with God. As we begin to experiment with telling God the truth about our abuse, about our feelings, about our terror, we can experience the reality that our feelings and our experiences will not destroy us, nor will they drive God away. United Church of Christ minister Jane Keene, in her liturgy for abuse survivors titled *A Winter's Song*, notes that we can speak before God "these forbidden things" and be assured of God's healing love.[6]

Building our relationship with God may also mean letting go of the expectation that God will make everything all right. The abuse still happened. The pain still exists. Crazy, sad, and evil things still occur in this world. But the prayers offered here come from the discovery that God stands with us in the midst of the pain. Our truth, spoken boldly, is at the heart of a true relationship with God. This is the lesson we find in Psalms, in Lamentations, in Jeremiah, and throughout biblical tradition. We can ask even the hardest question—God, where were you? Our God listens as we speak. God shares the anger and the outrage, and understands the fear and the sadness. God walks with us in recovery.

The invitation to relationship with God remains, at whatever level we are able to grasp it. We can turn to God and find a place for our pain, a place for our confusion, a place for our anger. With God we can experiment with telling the truth, and God, full of grace, can welcome the truth. Our God, full of truth and grace, is also full of love.

My God

My God walks with gentle steps,
My God talks with voice so soft,
My God dances gracefully,
My God holds the weak ones safe,
My God loves with mother love.
Fierce, protective, strong to save,
My God walks with gentle steps.
Nothing crushed by careless steps
when my God draws near.

Amen.

Daddies

Daddies hold their babies,
daddies hold them soft.
Strong daddy arms hold babies up
and gentle is the hold.

Daddies laugh with babies,
daddies smile with love.
Warm daddy eyes meet new eyes
and easy is the laugh.

Daddies care for babies,
keep them covered safe.
Big daddy hands reach baby hands
and tender is the care.

Daddies and their babies,
Eyes and arms and smiles and love.

Then a daddy hurt a baby
Baby cold with fear,
Baby crying new tears,
Baby frightened, lost.
No more smiles for baby,
No more shelter here.

And God, they call you Daddy,
God, they say you care.
Do you hold your babies?
Do you dry their tears?
Do you match them smile for smile?
Do you shelter safe?

God, that daddy stole your name.
God, that daddy made me mad.
God, I want a daddy back
(daddies hold their babies).
God, please daddy me.

Amen.

Mother God

You gather your children in your comforting arms.
Gather me close now.
You stand strong and protective, allowing no harm.
Like a bear with her cub, defend me now.
I have longed to know how you mother your children.
I have longed for your gentle love.
I have cried out for your safe, warm strength.
Mother, sweep away all that would keep me from you,
and rock me in your arms tonight.

Amen.

Keeper of Secrets

I have been a keeper of secrets. I have been alone.
I was told, "Tell no one." I was turned to stone.
I was tortured in silence. I was quiet, afraid.
He shouted "Shut up!" to my crying.
      He left me shattered, betrayed.

So I learned to keep my secret, learned my lessons well.
Learned "alone," learned "afraid," and learned how not to tell.
But God, your grace insists on truth, your love insists I speak.
And in my telling all, out loud, I grow strong where I was weak.

So hear each word. This happened. This man came to my bed.
I live no longer by his rules. Now I tell the world I bled.
Now I speak, for heaven's sake. Now I say it plain.
I will no longer be afraid, alone, in pain.

Now I'll say he lied to me. His words were never true.
And quietly, or quite out loud, I'll speak my truth to you.

Amen.

Splinters

The splinter in my finger hurts.
A sliver of glass runs deep.
The pain is there, at times dull and annoying,
at times quick and take-my-breath-away sharp.
Then I know it must come out.

The needle, hot and blue-black, made clean by fire.
The pain, sharp but healing.
And then relief, knowing true healing can begin.

This other pain inside me, God, is no small splinter,
but a broken part of me.
The pain is there,
at times dull and annoying,
at times quick and sharp.
And I know it must come out.

The white heat of your Truth and Love comes to me.
This is pain too, sharp and healing.
And now, relief?
And now, knowing true healing can begin?
Now true healing can begin.

Amen.

Honesty

God, I don't want to lie to you anymore.
What a scary thing, to stand true before Truth.
Now I'm me with you.
Me the one who screams with rage,
Me the angry one.
Me the one who often doubts,
Me the disappointed one.
Me the one who often weeps,
Me the honest one.
No more empty, self-protecting lies.
No more "I'm OK."
No more "I believe."
Just me, and "Help my unbelief."

Amen.

Jesus and the Children

Jesus, did you ever wonder which of those children
  you called to yourself had been abused?
Did you know them when they came to you,
eager for welcome, afraid to look up?
Did they know you when they came to you,
pulling your hand, climbing into your lap?
Did they wince in fear when you reached for them?
Did they know they were safe?

God, have you known me in those times when I came to you,
hoping for welcome, afraid to look up?
Because I know you,
somewhere inside me I know.
Even when I wince in fear, God, I know I'm safe.

Amen.

I Celebrate God's Grace

Well, this is the truth about what happened.
It really hurt. I was really scared.
And then I lost myself, for years.
I learned how to pretend so well that I forgot I was pretending.
I learned how to hide so well that I forgot where to find me.
I learned to mold myself so well that I forgot my form.
I forgot the truth.
Before you now I practice.
I practice my feelings, my form, myself.
I practice remembering.
I practice the truth.
And I celebrate your patience with the practicing.
I celebrate your grace.
I celebrate the space you've given me to learn.
And you reach me, as a searcher, with grace, with space, with love.

Amen.

Hiding

God, when I was a child I had to learn to hide. These were my
earliest lessons. I had to learn to hide completely, thoroughly.
I had to learn to keep any part of me from showing.
When he held me, I showed no pain.
When he searched for me, I lay low.
God, it was something I had to learn. It was hard,
    but I learned well.

Now I long to open myself to you.
Now I long to be found. Now I long to be held.
And you are the one who loves me just as I am.
I do not want to hide from you.
So as you seek me and as I run,
Know I had to learn my hiding lessons well.
Find me, God, with your ever-searching love.

Amen.

Questions

Mystery that seems beyond my knowing,
I grow weary with the question Why?
I grow weary with the question Where are you?
I grow weary with the anger and the sadness and the confusion.
I turn to you as Father and then run in fear.
Are you big enough for my anger, sadness, confusion, fear?
Today, can you heal my devastated soul?
Can you teach me something new?
Can you know me and not hate me? and not hurt me?
The link of pain and power makes me cringe
      when I hear of your power.
The link of pain and parent makes me cringe
      when they call you Parent.
You who would gather your people as a hen gathers her chicks,
      will you gather all these broken parts of me?
Can you teach, know, gather, gather, heal?

Brokenness

Once I took a broken toy
to my dad. Walked right up to him
toy in hand.
Looked up at him,
reaching out.
"Can you fix it?"
He carefully set aside his vodka and orange juice.
He stumbled slightly, eyes unfocused,
as he reached for my offering.
He took my small defenseless toy.
He worked to fix it, drunken hands
breaking it beyond repair.
When I tried to rescue it,
he pushed me away.
And I could do nothing to protect, to save
my fragile, broken toy.
God, at times my life feels broken
I bring this fragile life to you.
Walk right up to you, life in hand.
Can we fix it?
I hold my breath and wait to see what you will do.

How It Is Sometimes

God, this is how it is sometimes when I think about abuse.
The reality of children being hurt with no mighty command of
        STOP from you leads me to doubt you and to doubt myself.
When children are abused in your name and their cries are
        choked in their throats, where are you?
Am I not supposed to question? to cry? to hurt? to yell?
I have to tell you, this is something more than I can comprehend.

So there it is, God.

But I know that this can't be the whole picture. I know you stand
        with me in the pain. I know you can hear my rage and my fear.
Lead me deeper into your truth and grace and love.
Help me hold on through the storm, or help me know that you
        hold me when my own grip weakens.
And God, help me know that you are bigger than my pain and
        anger and fear and questions.

Amen.

Facing Feelings

Anger is a hard feeling for me to face. I have lived through anger storms, the rage of others crashing around me, down on me, until I could not stand, but bent low or crouched or huddled for protection. My own anger has howled within me, surging, straining for release, to break through, to destroy. I have heard of the wrath of God, a furnace blast that withers anything in its path.

God, anger is a hard feeling for me to face. I don't want to remember it. I don't want to acknowledge it. I don't want to talk about it. I push it down, only to feel its acid strength burn through any barrier I might place over it. I run from it and it pursues me.

God, I know you welcome me. I know you care. I know that you are not a god of rage. But this anger, God, that I bring with me, what shall we do with that?

I remember hearing once that the resurrection story was evidence that you could survive all the anger we humans can throw at you. Can you survive my anger, God? Will we endure? Because to know me, God, is to know not only my laughter and my gentleness but also the white-hot rage I carry within.

Amen.

Confession

Holy One,
I'm trying to sort through MY RESPONSIBILITIES.
Holy One, I'm trying to understand MY MISTAKES.
Holy One, I'm trying to figure out how to confess MY SINS
      to you.
I want my life back.
Let me tell you: when I was little, I was molested.
I didn't know that wasn't my responsibility. That wasn't my
mistake. That wasn't my sin.
And then things got confused. I couldn't remember how to love.
I made bad choices. I ran from you, from myself, from the pain.
I hurt people. I lashed out, or I simply held back. I got so mixed
up, and I couldn't find my way home.
I took no responsibility. I acknowledged no mistakes.
      I confessed no sin.
Now Holy One, I want MY LIFE back.
Protect me from my tendency to claim the guilt which is not
mine, and save me from my eagerness to deny the guilt which
is my own.
Holy One, hear my confession.

Amen.

Thinking I'm Something

"You really think you're something, don't you?" It's forbidden.
Me thinking I'm something, me caring for me, me feeling for me
      is forbidden. Liking myself is forbidden. Me listening to me—
      it isn't allowed.
"Who do you think you are?"
All-knowing God, how could you love me?
      Don't you know who I am?
Small, stupid, ugly, bad. Dirty, clumsy, dumb.
And inside, deep inside, there's something wrong with me.
How could you love me? Don't you know me?
Don't you know how scared I get? how sad? how selfish?
      how angry?
Wise One, if you know me, you can't love me.
Gracious One, if you love me, what do you know?
Yet your love breaks through, as you hold me close, as you look
      into my face and into my soul.
You look at me like an old friend, like someone you know well,
      like someone you know completely, and you say I love you.
You love me, and you know me, even better,
      even more than I know myself.
Give me strength to trust your knowing and your loving.
Give me courage to go on with the knowing,
in faith that it will lead to loving.
My soul runs from you. My self hides.
Will you say, "You really think you're something, don't you?"
Or are your words the ones I long to hear:
"I really think you're something. I'm really glad you're you."

Amen.

God Is Love

All the ways I look for love take me to the strangest places
turn me every different way, twist my heart in knots.
All the ways I search for love, looking into different faces
leave me aching, empty, low; waiting for the pain.
All the ways I long for love, all the ways I work for love,
all the earnings, all the yearnings tear my soul apart.
Then I found a different road, and I learned another way.
Love would seek me, love would find me,
     love was turning me.
Love would stay beside me watching, love would be there,
     always near.
Love would hold me keep me love me, love would welcome me.
No more earning, no more striving, no more "Am I good enough?"
Love is right here love inside me
love is waiting love beside me
love is teaching love surrounds me.
I am learning God is love.

Amen.

Celebration

I reach deep inside to find what is the heart of me.
Giver of Life, I celebrate the life you've given me.
I reject the pictures of destruction that so often fill my mind.
I celebrate the love you've given me.
I reject the pictures of hate that threaten to overwhelm
      all that I am.
I celebrate the body you have given me.
I reject the fear that has paralyzed this body.
The baby body that I had wasn't ready for the adult that hurt
      me. Now I work to let my grown-up body know that it's
      OK; that I can be completely in my body and be me.
God of all that is physical and all that is spiritual, help me see
      the connection, and heal, and rejoice.
I celebrate your gifts.

Amen.

Ordinary Day

Today is an ordinary day. I thank you, God, for the ordinary.
I thank you for a day of plain sunlight,
of simple tasks and easy mindless chores.
Sabbath God, I thank you for a day of rest.
No nightmares today.
No new growth today.
No terror today.
I thank you for this ordinary day.

Amen.

Sleep

God, some nights I lie awake looking up at the ceiling or staring
    at the clock, praying for sleep and holding on to my pillow
    and trying to hold on to your promises of comfort and care.
My mind goes back to other nights,
listening to arguments, listening for footsteps,
when I didn't want to sleep.
I thought my vigilance, the vigilance of a child,
could somehow stop the betrayal.
So God, tonight I cannot sleep.
I struggle to relax.
On nights like these, God, I need your presence, your comfort,
    your caring, your love.
On this night I need to know that you stand watch over those
    who tremble, and reach to wipe away each tear.
Tonight I cannot find a way to hold back thoughts and
    memories and fears.
So in my mind I add another picture, one of your protective love.
Tonight I am safe, even though my fears keep my heart pounding.
Tonight I breathe deep,
breathe in your peace and healing,
breathe out my fear and pain.
Be with me, God, tonight.

Amen.

Healing Touch

I have known a healing touch
A touch of warmth.
Not rough, but gentle.
Not demanding, but kind.

I have known a touch of love.
Not pain, not take, not hurt.
Not violating, but protecting, sheltering.
Not stripping away, but covering and caring.

I have known a comforting touch.
Not blaming not demanding not pushing not pulling.
Not holding on as I struggle to get away.

I have known a healing touch.
Could that be the hand of God?

The Long Walk Home

I remember clearly my first night in a group of childhood sexual abuse survivors. I sat quietly, surprised by my fears. I listened as the people in the group introduced themselves and as they each said something about the abuse they had suffered. As the group members spoke, I was also surprised by the connection I felt. I was amazed at how clearly I understood what these folks were talking about. They were describing my feelings, and I had never in my life heard anyone describe what was going on inside of me the way they did. For as long as I could remember I had felt like an outsider. I never felt like I belonged anywhere.

The image that came to my mind that night remains with me to this day. I felt as if I had been an exile all my life, and now I had finally stumbled into a group of people from my homeland. It was overwhelming. I hadn't even known that there were others who spoke my native tongue, and here I had discovered them. After all those years something really made sense and felt right. I was hearing new words that were also deeply familiar. I had found my way home.

The image of exiles returning home is a powerful one in Judaism and Christianity. We are all on a pilgrimage, and each one of us is learning to find the way. Abuse survivors have a place in this pilgrimage and truths to share with our fellow pilgrims. As we talk about abuse, we share needs, and possibilities, and truth. We talk about surviving, and we share strength and hope. Speaking to one another means sharing the pain and devastation and the journey of healing.

Child sexual abuse is an isolating experience. The assault itself nearly always occurs in secrecy. The child's cries are silenced with threats, both stated and implied. The emotions that follow create loneliness with which we live into adulthood. Most abuse survivors feel very alone.

The invitation to spiritual growth, on the other hand, is an invitation to connectedness. It is a call for exiles to come home. Spirituality connects us in profound ways with God, with other people, and with ourselves. The tension between our need to hide and the call to openness can be difficult to manage. As adults who were molested as children, we often find ourselves wondering where we belong, where home is.

The faith community is a pilgrim group. We are all wanderers who have come together to find power and comfort. Out of our uniqueness and our diversity, out of our own suffering and search for meaning, we bring gifts to each other. We need each other. Because many of us have spent our lives in invisible isolation chambers able to see out and able to be seen, yet still feeling separate and alone, we do not always recognize that we have something to offer the faith community. Learning to break through isolation into community and valuing what we bring with us can provide new dimensions of personal and spiritual growth.

The community of faith as a partner in this growth can be one of the places where we discover what it means to be part of a family. For many of us, the isolation we felt as a result of our abuse has kept us from knowing what community can mean. Unfortunately, there are some of us for whom the community of faith has been not a welcoming home, but a contributor to the abuse. Perhaps we told a person in our church what was happening, and we were not believed. Perhaps our abusers were church leaders, and there was no way our voices could be heard. We may have been told that the abuse was our fault or that all we had to do was "forgive" or "give it to God" and all would be well. In an attempt to avoid painful reality, some people may have said to us that for the sake of harmony we must remain silent and learn to move on.

Many of these experiences and responses reflect a significant misunderstanding of community. Community does not always mean harmony, and love does not always means peace. In order to create true community we must challenge false assumptions. Confronting painful reality will mean facing pain. Dealing with hard truths may be earthshaking. Yet it is out of such pain and struggle that truth is heard, honest relationships are built, and community is established.

Perhaps nowhere is such misunderstanding more clearly seen than in discussions of forgiveness. Misunderstanding forgiveness has permitted people to minimize the impact of child sexual abuse and to deny its devastating effects. The experience described by a friend of mine is a common one. She stated this: "Some years ago, when I told my family that I, like so many other children, had been molested, they referred me to the Bible, and they accused me of being in the wrong. When one of the men came to apologize, I could not accept it. It was too quick, too easy. Ten minutes of remorse, without knowing, or even wanting to know, what the consequences of his actions were. The apology seemed to be the only way for him to stop from having to hear what he had done to me."

The view of forgiveness as simple and easy has been presented to many abuse survivors, and it is important to recognize that *it is not accurate*. Forgiveness is not the same as forgetting, or pretending that an incident never happened, or minimizing its impact. Forgiveness is a part of a larger relational process of reconciliation that also involves confrontation and repentance. For example, Hebrew scriptures record a story of King David's sin against Bathsheba and Uriah. When the prophet Nathan confronted him with the sin, David saw the depth of the wrong and responded with deep sorrow. David understood and endured the consequences of his actions. It is at that point that his healing began.[1]

Repentance involves change, turning away from behavior that has harmed another and committing oneself to doing things differently.

Repentance means that one knows the impact of one's actions, understands the grievance held by the one who was wronged, and commits to whatever changes are necessary to behave differently.

I have seen the process of repentance at work in those who have abused children. It is not easy, and it is not quick. It is not accomplished by a simple "I'm sorry." Such repentance takes years, and it always includes listening and commitment to change. I have been in groups where adult survivors confront abusers and tell them of the impact of sexual assault on a child. Usually the abuser initially responds with denial or minimization. Sooner or later, however, if repentance and healing are to happen, the perpetrator must really hear the survivor and thus begin to understand the consequences of abuse. That is the beginning of growth. Like other aspects of spiritual growth, it does not happen all at once. The abuser must continue to listen and discover more and more layers of pain and deeper levels of repentance. Without the listening, no true reconciliation is possible.

After the abuser has listened to survivors, he or she must then learn, in painstaking and painful ways, to behave differently. The damage of the abuse must not be minimized, and its consequences cannot be dismissed. That is the spiritual work at hand for the abuser.

Understanding repentance and reconciliation in this way is helpful because it clarifies the role of forgiveness. To offer "forgiveness" before the pain has been articulated, the damage assessed, and the work of repentance completed is not the way to recovery. It does not clarify the injustice and it does not heal. To ask for "forgiveness" in a setting in which there has been no hearing and acceptance of the survivor's statements of pain, grief, and loss is a misuse of the word. To offer forgiveness to a perpetrator who has shown no willingness to listen and who has demonstrated no clear and radical change is to put other children at risk. Such actions do not create community. They do not bring about God's justice or God's love. They are inappropriate.

As survivors, we can reclaim ourselves and our power regardless of the actions of our abusers. They used us, blamed us, and belittled us. They defined our reality and then twisted that definition to fit their own purposes. They cut us off from true connectedness. When we cease to limit ourselves according to our abusers' perceptions and refuse to continue the abuse within ourselves, we are breaking the cycle of abuse. When we acknowledge our struggles in the light of our value as a part of God's loved creation, we are moving toward wholeness. This is our contribution to reconciliation. We break the silence in our faith community. Speaking the truth to each other in the same way we speak the truth to God brings healing, not only to ourselves but to the community as well. We speak the truth about pain and fear and anger so that truth can be known among us. We articulate our losses and our struggles, and those who wish to be in community can join their voices with us in support or in repentance.

In this discussion of reconciliation, it is helpful to remember that it may not be possible or even desirable to continue in relationship with the one who abused us. We may choose to confront our abusers for the sake of our own healing. Such a confrontation, however, is not required for growth. We cannot expect that such a confrontation will necessarily lead to repentance. We may never get the response we want from the ones who hurt us. The key in all these choices is to remember that there is no "required" way to approach this aspect of healing or community-building. Confrontation is not a requirement for personal or spiritual growth. It is a very individual choice. There is no "should" attached to this aspect of community.

As we survivors learn to set limits, as we discover new ways of relating to ourselves and others, as we develop new tools for living, our healing will continue. This healing does not depend on the action of someone else, but comes from within ourselves. Our *healing* is our way of limiting the power of abuse in our lives. In healing we are counteracting the power of the abuse and the abuser in our lives. The pain is not denied. The scars are still there. The difference is that we have spoken our truth, have bandaged our wounds, and have reclaimed our souls.

So we continue our healing and our journey toward home. Although talking to God about child sexual abuse is a very personal matter, with private feelings to share, private memories to work through, and a private, personal relationship to build, we are also called to relationships with others. Spiritual healing can also come as we break through isolation to discover connectedness. It may include learning the meaning of belonging to a faith community.

As a community we shape one another's perceptions, offer support and hope, and raise our voices for healing and for justice. The community of faith has certainly given many of us a faith perspective and has shaped our relationship with God. For some of us, that community has also been a source of pain, rejection, or even more abuse. As a community, therefore, we need to talk to each other and to God about child sexual abuse. We need to learn about connectedness and we need to speak out about human significance, even in the face of suffering. As a community, we need to heal.

Pilgrims

Mystery, who calls me through the pain,
the loneliness, the terror,
Strong Deliverer, who reaches past my fears,
Eternal Friend, who catches and holds
    when I can hold no longer,
hear my prayer.
I ask for direction when I feel only aimlessness;
when my wandering in this wilderness has convinced me
    that I will never find a Promised Land.
I ask for guidance as I return from exile,
as I work to follow your voice and find my way home.
I ask for protection as I discover that I can
    let go of this shame I have carried,
and I find in you promise and love and
    warm welcome and home.

Amen.

Refusing to Move On

A scar is a scar. It doesn't go away.
The broken bone may be set, but in the healing,
    traces of the injury remain.
There it is.
I was abused. I was hurt. And a scar is a scar.

People around me say, "Forgive."
Those who know nothing about brokenness and healing
    say to me, "Move on."
Those who fear the pain say, "Don't look back."
I insist on acknowledging this pain.
I insist on recognizing the scar.
I insist on remembering why there is this jagged, thin line.
I insist on being here with me, on holding me, on saying,
    "That was wrong."

Jesus, I know that you remember your pain.
You still carry those scars that Thomas touched
    with his doubting.
You insist that there was a real cost when you were hurt.
Stand with me in this place of remembering.
Stand with me as I clarify: Real injury means real pain.
Stand with me in this truth: A scar is a scar.

Amen.

Therapy and God

The sound of voices comes from the room next door.
Children's voices.
A car starts, then drives away.
I sit very still, not moving. Listening.
I sit remembering, then forgetting what I just remembered.
A woman sits across from me. Also listening.
The room is very quiet. Only the sounds outside, crowding in.
Only the muffled sounds, amplified in my head, amplified by my
shallow breathing, amplified by my terror.
Don't move, don't move. Just be still until the terror passes.
My gentle God, I ask you to join us in this room.
Hear the stories I tell. Hear the silence,
        words I cannot even whisper yet.
Hear her gentle questions that explore the pain.
Be with me when I freeze in fear.
Be with me when I cry out from remembered forgotten anguish.
Be with me when I rage, when I strike out,
        when my fist squeezed tight
swings into the nothing that is now in front of me.
Be with me when it seems that healing will never come.
Be with me when I wonder where you were.
Be with me when I wonder where you are.
Be with me as I heal.

Amen.

Accountability

God, I hold them accountable. Those people who hurt children,
I hold them accountable.

God, I hold you accountable too. Even in all the ways I have
trusted you, I also have to ask, Where were you? Where
are you?

Hear my anger and my confusion. Hear my cries for justice. Hear
my cries for children.

God, redeem this world and abolish this crime.

God, I hold you accountable. Help us now hold each other
accountable, too, until we find a way for justice and grace
to rule our world, for children to be safe, and for your will
to be done on earth as it is in heaven.

Amen.

Survival

O holy one,
Sometimes I am amazed to have made it through another day.
Another day of pain, of wondering if I can keep going.
Another day of memories and tears.
Another day of healing.

O gentle one,
As I now relax into the evening,
as I now relax into my own survival,
as I now prepare to make it through another night,
be with me in my sleeping, in my dreaming.
Be with me in the darkness that once held pain and terror,
and now holds only night.
Be with me.
Let your presence assure me that I am not alone.

There was a time when only alone was safe.
But, God, I got so lonely.
Now I'm learning I can be safe with you.

Amen.

Old Tears

These tears I'm crying now are old tears formed decades ago
    in my childhood, when tears were forbidden.
I kept them inside, waiting for safety.
The wall that held them back was built of threats, of fear, of pain.
The water in these tears has almost dried up.
The salt has almost crystallized with age,
eaten through my soul,
purified my wounds.
Now the healing has begun, and now my tears can fall.
And now, my comforter, I cry these tears.
Now they fall freely.
Now their falling brings freedom.
And you, my comforter, are the one who gathers my tears, who
    hears my pain, who holds me gently as I sob, who dries
    my face.
You are the one who guards me as I grieve.
For healing, for safety, for love, I give you thanks.

Amen.

Ways to Care

When I look at children, I realize there are so many ways
    to hurt them.
Humiliate them. Embarrass them. Outwit them.
    Overpower them.
There are so many ways to injure children. Outmaneuver them.
    Break them.
There are so many ways to cripple them, twist them,
    blame them.
God, so many ways to destroy them.
And loving Mother, I struggle to learn, what are the ways
    to love a child?
Strengthen a child, empower a child, lift up a child,
    believe a child.
Loving Mother, help me learn, help us learn the ways to care,
    to nurture,
to love the children around us and the children within us.

Amen.

For Others Who Cry

Sometimes it's more than my own pain that hurts.
Sometimes I think of others who cry, who tremble,
who call out to you.

When I was little, people told me you blessed little children.
I could only turn to you, expecting salvation, expecting
      immediate relief.
The prayers of a little child go unanswered.
Hands of a little child, folded in prayer, are pulled apart
and forced into other foldings.

These little ones too might hear of your love.
How will they love when the love they know now is such pain?
Their daddies mommies brothers uncles aunts who say
      "I love you"
have mixed those words with pure pain.
Their teachers preachers elders deacons who say "God is love"
have mixed those words with deep fear.

Be with us all as we sort through those words,
picking carefully among the sharp edges of brokenness
to find the pieces of love, of truth, of you.

Amen.

To the Community of Faith

There was a knife in me.
Now I bleed all over my soul.
If you get too close to me, I might bleed on you.
I sit among the people of God.
I sit among them, bleeding.
What will they do with all this pain?
Will they turn their heads from me?
Will they move away from the red splattering?
Will they cry out in disgust?
Or will they make bandages and gently cover my wounds?
Will they understand?

For WG

Today I got a phone call, and I learned my friend is dead.
She couldn't go on living in the nightmare of her memories.
She couldn't go on seeking, and wondering if you hate her.
When she reached for the light, she couldn't see you shining.
When she called out for help, she never heard your answer.
And so she chose to end the struggle by ending her life.
When I heard, I was so angry. Angry about the pain, the hurt,
    the evil done to her. I didn't want to talk to anyone. I
    didn't want to talk to you.
And now, God, I don't know what to say to you about my friend.
She struggled so long, she hurt so much.
The ones who hurt her taught her lies about you, told her she
    was evil, tried to twist her spirituality into knots that
    bound her.
So she was left with fears, with doubts, with a shattered self.
And now she's gone.
Please catch her in your mother arms and hold her safe at last.
Please teach her now what life was never able to teach her,
    that you care and comfort and love.
And as I stand before you, mourning and remembering,
give me courage to live my life in you,
give me integrity to speak the truth,
and grant me grace to continue to survive.

Amen.

What I Hope

God, I hope for healing.
I hope for tenderness in touching.
I hope for peaceful days, for quiet nights.
I hope for children to be safe.
I hope the cycle will be broken.
I hope people will learn to care.
I hope injured people will find hope.
Faith, hope, and love abide.
God, I hope that's true.

Amen.

Repentance

I listened to a child molester speak today.
I heard his words of denial, mixed with words of insight
about the pain he had caused in a young child's life.
He talked about what he had done,
and then he stopped. He hung his head.

When I reached out to him,
it was not to deny the devastation he had caused
or to pretend that recovery would be quick.
I just wanted him to know that on his long journey,
he was taking a first step.
The truth he spoke, which must have seemed to him like
the end of everything,
was really a beginning of hope and healing.

God of justice and of grace,
stay near him as he does the hard work of repentance:
learning to listen to the truth of his assault,
learning to speak the truth to himself,
learning to speak the truth to you,
Learning to change.

And God, stand with the child he hurt. Bring that child to a
place of love and life, where the story can be told. Let that child
find those who let children talk, and who hear and believe.

Amen.

Forgiveness

I don't know what to do with "forgiveness."
When I think about it, I'm confused. When I check my feelings,
 I'm angry and afraid.
Too many people have given false images and false information.
"Forgive and forget" have been linked. But all I know about
 healing and all I know about you tells me that such a link
 does not lead to healing.
I have needed to remember my pain. When I forget,
 I am paralyzed with fear.
I have needed to remember my terror. When I forget,
 my anxiety overwhelms me.
I have needed to remember my anger. When I forget,
 I am trapped in a cycle of despair.

Forgiveness. What does that mean? Mostly I know what it isn't.
I know it isn't pretending everything is fine. I know it cannot
mean that life can just continue on unchanged. This wrong that
was done has cost so much, and I know that forgiveness will not
mean ignoring the cost.

God of grace, your forgiveness starts with the naming of the sin.
Will this perpetrator name his sin? Is he willing to acknowledge
what his careless, selfish action did? Will he listen to the cost?

God of grace, lead me to the place where I can choose what power
will guide my life. Never to forget. Only to take the next step.
May I live by the power of love, as it heals me and sets me free.

Amen.

A Prayer to Keep Going

God, I need you.
Carry me when I'm weak, hold me when I'm tired.
Love me when I cannot care anymore.
And when I huddle, lonely and afraid,
cover me with your strong, protective hands,
guard my sleep,
and wake me gently in the morning,
rested and strong,
and ready to try again.

Amen.

Newborn Blessing

Creator of new life, we pray a blessing for newborn children.
Their world is just beginning; their eyes just barely focus on this
    not yet familiar place.
Creator, we pray a blessing.
Strengthen us to speak the truth in a world that might not
    want to hear.
Help us to keep talking until the truth is heard.
We the people of faith must find a way to keep the children safe.
We must find the courage to change our dangerous world.
Creator, please bless this newborn child, now resting in my arms.
And bless us too, with restlessness, until all children rest safe.

Amen.

Teacher

Jesus, they call you rabbi, teacher.
So teach me, Jesus, about survival.
Teach me to keep believing, to keep holding on.
Teach me how to refuse to allow abuse done to me
    to determine the limits of my life and of my love.
Rabbi, teach me about recovery. Show me how your healing care
    can bind the deepest wounds.
Teach me how to turn the fear and pain into power and
    strength, tools for living as myself, open and honest and
    whole.
And teach me, rabbi, about community. Lead me into a healing
    place of welcoming arms and sheltering harbor.
Bring me home, to a family you have created,
    governed by a law of love.
Let us speak out against abuse and keep the children safe.
So teach me, rabbi, about you,
my wounded healer, my strong deliverer,
my faithful friend, my God.

Amen.

Giving Thanks

God,
I rejoice in all the ways you embrace hurting people.
When I wrestle with the unknowable, I know you stand with me.
When I struggle with the unspeakable, you hear me.
When my fears threaten to overwhelm me, you strengthen me.
When the phantom pain of lost possibilities and stolen hopes
strikes the deepest part of me, you are my comfort.

When my heart soars with the joys of healing, you dance beside me.
When I discover new beginnings and new truths,
you gather me in your arms to complete the circle.

And for this faithfulness, which I still don't understand,
and for this steadfastness, which breaks through
    my own clouds of doubt,
and for this grace, which is crowned by love,
I give you thanks.

Amen.

Confrontation

God, today I choose to face the one who injured me.
As I look into those eyes that showed no mercy to me,
give me strength to speak the truth.
As I stand up to the one who towered over me and called forth
    all my fears,
give me courage to stand firm.
And let my actions be chosen by me:
to be who I am and not what this one who hurt me would have
    me to be;
to believe my truth and not the words of the one who lied to me
    for so long.
As I wonder where today might lead, lead me on.

Amen.

God of Children's Laughter

God of children's laughter, I pray for healing times.
Let our love bring laughter back to children who were hurt.
May your healing presence bless us, fill our lives,
    and let us laugh.
God of children's tears, I pray for comforting times.
Let our love create a place of safety for the weeping ones.
May we break the cycle of abuse, in our lives and in
    our children's lives.
In a world that turns away so often from hurting children,
    may we have the courage to stand and the endurance to
    work for change,
until all your children laugh and cry safely in loving arms.

Amen.

A Little Prayer

Today I pray a little prayer,
the words from deep inside of me.
A prayer to set me free.

Today I cry a little while,
the tears that fall may bring release.
Today I seek your peace.

Today I say a little bit,
I tell you something of the pain,
more than these words contain.

Today I heal a little more,
I feel your warmth that strengthens me.
Today you set me free.

Amen.

Conclusion: The Journey Goes On

As we find the courage and the words to talk to God about child sexual abuse, we will continue to heal and grow. We will discover a resource for recovery that empowers us and also brings power to the faith community. There is still so much to tell God and each other. There is still so much to ask. This is not a process that comes to an end. As with any spiritual pilgrimage, healing is an ongoing journey of stretching, seeking, connecting, and becoming whole.

It seems to me that life was never meant to be completely understood. Individuals throughout history have tackled the task of explaining human existence, and what they have encountered inevitably is mystery. We face that mystery when we ask the question Why? We face it when we struggle to understand child sexual abuse or to explain our survival. We meet the mystery when we talk to God about our abuse, and wonder about God's presence and protection, and express doubts and anger, and find healing. In our encounters with ourselves, with others, and with God, we certainly find clues to the mystery. The full picture, however, is never known.

There are important things we *can* know. We can know that what happened to us was not our fault, and we can work to let go of our guilt and shame. We can know that there are ways of being in the world that can enable us to move past our fears. We can find power and purpose and connection and wholeness. We can speak to God about our abuse, and we can find healing as we give voice to our reality.

Like others who have confronted evil, we cannot come to a full understanding of the presence of evil in the world or of the power of evil to hurt the innocent. And so we are left with decisions of faith. As we acknowledge our human limitations, we are invited to experience the limitlessness of God. As we work to create a community of faith where children are heard, pain is honored, and healing can happen, we experience the power of God. As survivors, we can find comfort and courage in the presence of God. We can discover freedom as our sorrow turns to joy and our weakness becomes strength. This is a paradox, a puzzle. We experience the dichotomy of separateness and connectedness—the celebration of our unique significance in the world and the joy of community. We cannot explain the mystery, but we can live it. We can keep talking to God about child sexual abuse. Amen.

Prayers I Still Need

When I come to the end of my prayers, I find that there are
    prayers I still need.
A prayer for the courage to speak the truth.
Another prayer for the pain.
A prayer for the sadness.
A prayer for fears.
A prayer for the anger that sometimes smolders
    and sometimes burns.
A prayer for justice and for grace.
A prayer for strength to keep telling my story,
to keep moving toward wholeness, to keep moving toward you.
A prayer for wisdom.
Another prayer for love.

Amen.

Notes

1. Moving toward Wholeness

1. Maya Angelou, *I Know Why the Caged Bird Sings* (New York: Random House, 1969), 84.
2. Victor Frankl, *Man's Search for Meaning* (Boston: Beacon Press, 1992).
3. Ellen Bass and Laura Davis, *The Courage to Heal: A Guide for Women Survivors of Child Sexual Abuse* (New York: Harper & Row, 1988), 159.
4. Marie Marshall Fortune, *Sexual Violence, The Unmentionable Sin* (New York: Pilgrim Press, 1983), xiii.
5. Bass and Davis, *The Courage to Heal*, 156.

2. God Who Walks with Us

1. Alice Walker, *The Color Purple* (New York, Simon & Schuster, Inc.), 1982.
2. David Heller, "The Children's God," *Psychology Today* (December 1985): 24.
3. Russell Baker, *Growing Up* (New York: NAL Dutton, 1992), 61.
4. Bass and Davis, *The Courage to Heal*, 157.
5. 1 John 4:18a
6. Jane Keene, *A Winter's Song* (New York: Pilgrim Press, 1991), xi.

3. The Long Walk Home

1. 2 Samuel 11–12.